Depression

A guide to managing and overcoming depression

TIM WATKINS
For
LIFE SURFING

ISBN-13: 978-1492391302
ISBN-10: 1492391301

CONTENTS

Life Surfing

What is depression?

Depression is more than simply feeling down or unhappy. It is a medically diagnosable condition that can seriously undermine your health and wellbeing.

Symptoms

The common symptoms of depression are:

- Ongoing sadness and low mood
- Feelings of helplessness and hopelessness
- Tearfulness
- Problems with sleep
- Poor concentration and forgetfulness
- Loss of enjoyment
- Loss of sex drive
- Changes in appetite and weight (usually loss of appetite and weight loss)
- Feeling anxious or worried
- Thoughts of self-harm or suicide.

Other less common or less obvious symptoms include:

- Physical aches and pains
- Headaches
- Digestive problems
- Constipation
- Changes to the menstrual cycle.

If you have several of these symptoms to the point that they are interfering with your daily life, for more than a fortnight, you may want to discuss these with your doctor. If you have thoughts of suicide or self-harm, we advise you to see your doctor. You might also want to talk confidentially to the Samaritans 08457 90 90 90.

Warning signs

Although not strictly "symptoms" of depression, warning signs can act as an early indication of the onset of depression. Warning signs can include any change in behaviour, but commonly include:

- Using drugs like alcohol, caffeine and nicotine
- Comfort eating
- Losing interest in your appearance (or becoming obsessively well turned out)
- "Being busy" – using a lot of energy, but not actually getting things done
- Withdrawing from social activities (making excuses to avoid people)
- Developing a negative or pessimistic outlook on life
- Struggling at work, school or college
- Becoming forgetful.

While it may be tempting to think that depression is simply something you can work through or snap out of, such an approach can cause real difficulties. Left untreated, depression can seriously undermine your social life; removing your ability to function in employment, disrupting your relationships, and destroying your social life.

While there are many things you can do for yourself to promote recovery from depression, it will not hurt to visit your GP. Your doctor may want to do some simple blood tests to rule out an underlying physical illness, and may be able to offer access to a range of early interventions as well as medication if your depression is severe enough for this to be necessary.

Life Surfing

Understanding Wellbeing

A helpful model for understanding wellbeing is the image of someone pushing a burden along a slope. There are three factors that affect the ease or difficulty:

o   The angle of the slope (is it steep or shallow?) is about the wider environmental, political and economic conditions within which we live.

o   The traction of the slope (is it firm or slippery?) represents the various institutions within which we live our lives. These include our families, neighbourhoods, workplaces, schools and colleges, clubs and associations, etc.

o   The burden (is it light or heavy?) is about how we are as individuals. It includes our skills and abilities, our beliefs and thoughts, our emotions, our physical bodies, and the way we interact socially.

Someone who has maximum positive wellbeing will be fully engaged socially (at work, at home, in their local community and at play); physically healthy; emotionally balanced, rational and considered; and utilising their core skills and abilities. Their lives will be lived in supportive, nurturing families, neighbourhoods, schools, colleges, workplaces and social associations. These will function within a benign environment, in a free society that delivers economic prosperity and social cohesion.

Of course, few people ever enjoy such a blessed life. Most of humanity is excluded from the benign political and economic conditions enjoyed in Western Europe and the USA in the decades after 1945. Even in these societies, there is no guarantee that social institutions will be nurturing and empowering. Too many people in the UK live in broken families, attend failing schools and live in neighbourhoods where crime and antisocial behaviour are too high. Too many employers create and maintain bullying, pressurising, target-driven management cultures that make work insecure and unhealthy for employees.

Nor should we ignore inequalities in health. People born in the UK's poorest communities are shorter, more prone to chronic illness and disability, and likely to die 10 years earlier than those born in the wealthiest areas.

Someone with depression is likely to have to struggle with personal factors. Their depression will result in:

- Social withdrawal (possible ending in unemployment)
- Deteriorating physical health, including:
    - Disrupted sleep
    - Digestive problems
    - Pain
    - Poor diet
    - Lack of exercise
- Poor, often negative, emotional and mental health
- Frustrated core skills and abilities.

Since most depression is reactive, these problems are often the result of wider social problems such as:

- Difficulties at work
- Relationship problems
- Being a victim of crime or antisocial behaviour
- Being a carer for a friend or relative.

Depression may also be the result of wider economic factors such as:

- Debt
- Redundancy
- Unemployment
- Poverty
- Homelessness.

Nor are these factors only the cause of depression. In many cases, they also result from depression. So, for example, someone may become depressed after being made redundant. This causes them to withdraw socially, and begins to affect their whole outlook on life. This may result in their relationships breaking down, and may cause them to lose their home. The combination of this will make their depression worse, making it even harder for them to rebuild their lives.

Recovery from depression means taking steps across all of these areas of your life. This means both cutting back on things that make your depression worse, and engaging with things that improve your wellbeing.

Seen in this way, decisions about both treatment and self-help can be taken in terms of whether they improve or worsen your wellbeing.

Treatments

In England and Wales, access to NHS treatments for depression are via your local General Practitioner (GP) service.

GPs can offer a range of evidence-based treatments for depression that have been recommended by the National Institute for Health and Clinical Excellence (NICE).

NICE recommend a "stepped care" approach to the treatment of depression based on the severity of the condition and the impact of treatment.

In mild cases of depression, NICE recommend a range of early interventions including:

- o Books on prescription
- o Exercise on prescription
- o Computerised Cognitive Behavioural Therapy (CCBT)
- o Brief Structured Counselling
- o Guided Self-help.

Where these approaches do not succeed, or in more moderate cases of depression, NICE recommend more traditional medical approaches such as:

- o Antidepressant drugs
- o Counselling
- o Cognitive Behavioural Therapy (CBT)

    o   Psychological ("talking") therapies.

Where people do not respond to these approaches, or where depression is severe, the GP will make a referral to a Community Mental Health Team, who are approved by NICE to deliver more intense treatments such as:

- o Combinations of medications
- o A broader range of psychological and occupational therapies
- o Day care
- o Social support
- o In-patient care.

In a small number of cases, Electro Convulsive Therapy (ECT) may be used, although this tends to be reserved for people whose depression is particularly severe (for example, to the point where they are unable to feed themselves) and where other approaches have not worked.

Antidepressants are readily available. Most of the Prozac-type (Selective Serotonin Reuptake Inhibitor) antidepressants cost less than £5.00 for a month's supply. As such, there is no real constraint on GPs prescribing these.

Other treatments and services are in shorter supply. In Wales, books and exercise on prescription are free national schemes. In England, availability depends on whether a trust or practice has bought into a scheme. On the other hand, talking therapies (primarily CBT) are much more widely available in England than in Wales.

Access to brief structured counselling and computerised CBT will depend on whether an individual practice is prepared to fund these.

You should bear in mind that the NHS is not the only provider of talking therapies:

- o Many employers provide Employee Assistance Programmes that include telephone counselling
- o Some private insurance policies include cover for psychological support
- o Voluntary counselling services are available in some areas
- o Private counselling and psychological therapies are readily available (at a price).

It is certainly worth exploring what is available in your area if the alternative is a long wait for NHS provision.

Life Surfing

Alternative and complementary therapies

One of the problems with NHS treatments for depression is that they are not always effective. For example, antidepressants only work for 60 to 70 percent of users, while talking therapies are effective in less than 50 percent of patients.

In such circumstances, there has been strong demand for alternative and complementary approaches.

Usually, alternative treatments are even less effective than medicine. However, in the case of depression, there is a herbal remedy—St. John's Wort—which has been well researched, and shown to be at least as effective as antidepressants in the treatment of mild-moderate depression.

It is important not to take terms like "herbal", "natural" or "alternative" as meaning safer or better than the medicine prescribed by your GP. St. John's Wort is unusual in having undergone clinical trials. Most herbal/natural/alternative remedies have not been subjected to such rigorous testing. And even St. John's Wort has side effects, and is dangerous if taken together with another antidepressant.

It is advisable to talk to your GP or pharmacist before taking an alternative medicine.

Complementary therapies are different insofar as they do not interfere with any medicines or therapies that you may be using. Although the evidence for the effectiveness of complementary therapies is weak (largely because the research has not been conducted), there is some evidence that several complementary therapies can help with depression because they promote relaxation and improved physical wellbeing.

Hands-on therapies like aromatherapy, massage, reflexology and shiatsu may be of considerable benefit solely in terms of the relief from anxiety and stress and the promotion of relaxation and sleep that many users experience. As such, even though these therapies may not represent a "cure" for depression, they may help to bring about recovery.

Exercise programmes like Pilates, Tai Chi and Yoga have also been shown to promote relaxation and wellbeing, and so may also be used to complement formal treatment.

Self-help

If you return for a moment to our model of someone pushing a burden along a slope, you may notice that even though many of the things that cause, trigger or exacerbate depression are properties of the slope, medical treatment is limited to addressing the burden. Indeed, outside specialist mental health services, treatment is about addressing just three areas of your personal burden:

- o Physical symptoms
- o Emotions
- o Thoughts and beliefs.

So, for example, you might take an antidepressant to help you sleep (physical) and improve your mood (emotions), and you might see a counsellor to improve your negative feelings (emotions), thoughts and beliefs.

Looked at in this way, self-help is about additionally addressing all of those things that treatment excludes. Self-help addresses the burden more holistically, and it does not shy away from addressing the slope.

Shrinking the burden

Depression can be thought of as a form of disengagement at every level of your being:

- Social withdrawal – you lose interest in people whose company you used to enjoy and the things you used to do
- Physical health – you disengage from physical activity, fitness levels fall, your sleep is disrupted, you feel exhausted
- Posture – your back and shoulders hunch as you curl forward
- Diet – you lose your appetite and develop a taste for heavily flavoured food (some of us also comfort eat)
- Feelings – you become "numb" to the full range of emotions, but continue to experience sadness, shame and guilt
- Thoughts – your thoughts slow down, so decision making becomes difficult; you become more negative; you worry excessively
- Beliefs – you lose faith in the future, and may no longer have meaning in your life
- Impaired abilities—symptoms of poor memory and concentration, impaired motor function, and thinking that you are inadequate or useless may stop you doing the things that you are good at and that you most enjoy.

Each of these is a process rather than an event, and can go on for months before you realise that something is wrong.

Each is also a vicious circle that causes depression to worsen. For example, the less you engage in physical activity, the more unfit you become, and the less you feel like being physically active.

A large part of recovery from depression is about reversing these downward spirals.

Avoid quick fixes

These processes are often compounded by "quick-fixing" - using substances and behaviours that make you feel good in the short-term, but make your depression worse in the longer-term.

We commonly turn to five substances to help us cope with stress:

- o Alcohol
- o Caffeine
- o Chocolate
- o Nicotine
- o Sugar.

With the exception of smoking (to obtain nicotine) these are relatively harmless when used occasionally to help overcome short-term stress. However, when these are used as a response to prolonged stress, anxiety and depression, their inevitable over-use causes serious health problems that compound depression.

Less often, people over-use illegal, prescription and over-the-counter drugs in an attempt to overcome the symptoms of stress, anxiety and depression. These will also have a negative impact on your health in the longer-term.

In addition to using substances to help cope with stress, many of us turn to a range of quick fix behaviours such as:

- Comfort eating
- Compulsive exercising
- Shopping beyond what you can afford
- Gambling
- Casual sex
- Over-working.

These are behaviours that we will have learned make us feel better in the short-term. However, in the long-term they will have a negative effect not only on your wellbeing but also socially.

Your quick fixes can be a warning sign that you are becoming depressed or that your depression is worsening. For example, if you are someone who uses caffeine to help you get going in the mornings, and you (or someone close to you) notice that your coffee consumption has gone up, this could be a sign that your mood and energy levels are deteriorating.

There isn't a magic bullet!

One reason for much of the discontent with formal treatments for depression is that a medical understanding of recovery may be different to your own desired outcome.

For many people in the early 1990s, the apparent benefit of the so-called "wonder drug" *Prozac* was its promise to improve mood and energy levels without the need to change. The marketing hype seemed to suggest that you could live a stressful, chaotic lifestyle (of the kind we now know is a major cause of depression), and a daily dose of *Prozac* would prevent you becoming depressed.

We now know that *Prozac* isn't a wonder drug. Rather, it acts in a similar manner to a plaster cast on a broken limb—giving you some additional support while you recover. Nevertheless, many people still seek to live stressful, chaotic and unhealthy lifestyles, but want not to have to live with the negative consequences.

This has allowed many charlatans and snake oil salesmen to sell all manner of untested alternative treatments for depression. It has also led to a great deal of over-exaggeration of the benefits of medical treatments such as CBT, which has filled the gap left by our disillusionment with antidepressant drugs.

The truth is that if a chaotic, stressful and unhealthy lifestyle and/or unhealthy life circumstances are behind your depression, you will not find the solution in pills, potions and therapies. The only route to recovery is in addressing your life circumstances, adopting a less chaotic and stressful lifestyle, and opting for a range of healthier lifestyle choices.

Treatments and therapies may help you to achieve this. But in and of themselves, they will not bring about recovery from depression.

Don't be afraid to ask for help

Addressing the circumstances that underlie your depression often has to involve help and support from others.

Depression is often triggered by life events and situations that either involve loss and change (e.g., redundancy), or result in you being stuck in unpleasant circumstances (e.g., a relationship breakdown). Where these situations are ongoing, they can cancel out the beneficial effects of any treatment or self-help that you are using to help you overcome your depression.

You do not have to face these situations alone. Indeed, there are many organisations that can offer information, advice and support to people in your situation. A useful starting point is the DirectGov website (www.direct.gov.uk) which contains information about all of the support and advice offered by government as well as links to external organisations that can help.

Understand *your* depression

Although it is possible to talk about depression in general, each of us experiences the condition differently. What causes one person to get worse may not affect another. Similarly, what helps some people recover may not work for you. So it is important to start learning how *your* depression operates.

A starting point for doing this is to learn as much as possible about depression, and relate this to your own experiences of the condition.

Self-monitoring is a useful approach to understanding the subtleties of *your* depression. Some people will keep a mood diary in which they record how they feel, what they thought about, and what they did during the day. Alternatively, you might want to keep weekly self-monitoring records using a form on which you can monitor things like your mood and energy level against a range of things that might have an effect on these such as how much sleep you got, the things you did in the day, whether you used too much alcohol and whether you ate healthy food.

You can find out more about depression on the www.depressiononline.org website, which also contains free self-management tools including a self-management form. The site is free, but you will need to log in to download the free resources.

Plan ahead

Whether you are doing something as complex as organising the Olympic Games or something as simple as going to the shops, you have to plan. The difference is that with the simpler things, our planning tends to be done in our heads. So, ordinarily, you might make a mental list of things you need to buy and of the shops you will need to visit to get them. You may need to think about transport—will you drive, catch a bus or walk? You may have a contingency plan in case you cannot find the things you want to buy.

Remember that depression undermines memory and concentration. This means that these internal plans will not work. It is most likely that you will forget things or not be able to do them properly. This, in turn, will leave you with a low mood, a sense of failure and the thought that you are useless.

In some cases—like shopping—a plan might be little more than a list of shops you need to visit with a sub-list of the items you want to buy. Other, more ambitious projects—like finding a new job—might involve more detailed planning. However, the process of planning can give you a better understanding of the things you will need to do to achieve your goal.

Small steps

It is common for people with depression to ignore the impact of the condition on their ability to achieve their goals. All too often, we try to achieve the same kind of results we would have achieved when we were well. This is known as setting yourself up to fail.

Breaking goals down into small, manageable tasks is the key to avoiding this. For example, your goal might be to "clean my house". This is far too big a task to complete in one go. If you try to clean your house from top to bottom, you will exhaust yourself with the result that your depression will be worse for days or even weeks. You will also leave yourself feeling that you have failed, and beating yourself up for not doing more.

Suppose, instead, that you broke "cleaning my house" into manageable tasks such as:

o   Wash the dishes
o   Pick up clutter in the living room
o   Take old clothing to the charity shop
o   Make the beds.

Some of these tasks (e.g., wash the dishes) will be achievable quite quickly. Others (e.g., take clothes to the charity shop) might be the only thing that you do for one day.

It might take you weeks to complete the goal of cleaning the house, but planning and breaking things down into manageable tasks will allow you to record your successes.

Half-finished tasks are a good sign!

When someone is really depressed, it is common to find that lots of household chores and tasks have not even been started. When someone is well, many of them will be completed. But when someone is truly recovering from depression, you will see lots of incomplete tasks. For example, you may find that the ironing board is out but there is still ironing to do; the vacuum cleaner is in the middle of the room; some dishes are clean but others wait in the sink; part of the lawn has been mown, but some still needs cutting.

This is good because it means that this person has learned the art of stopping before they over-tire themself. A depressed person will try to do all of the things that they could do before they became ill. But their depression will cause them to get tired much more quickly. If they get too tired, their mood and energy levels will sink for days and weeks to come.

Someone who is recovering will feel themselves getting tired and will stop to rest. To begin with, this will involve far more time spent resting than being active. But by doing this, they gradually build their energy levels and improve their mood. As the days and weeks pass, they find that they can do more before they get tired. Eventually, they are once again able to do the things they could do before they became depressed. But it requires patience.

Building personal resilience

Building your personal resilience means adopting healthy lifestyle changes at every level of your being:

- o Social engagement
- o Physical health
- o Emotional well being
- o Thoughts and beliefs
- o Core skills and abilities.

Social engagement

Depression affects your ability to function socially. It impairs your concentration, memory and motor functions which in turn affect your performance at work. It also leaves you tired, making you less likely to engage socially and more likely to withdraw into your home or even under your duvet.

Unfortunately, withdrawal makes you even more susceptible to depression. So it is easy to get into a vicious downward spiral. The only way of reversing this is to engage socially even if you don't feel like it.

The trick is not to overdo things. So, for example, going out to a quiet café, restaurant or bar with a friend is better than going to a busy, noisy club.

Physical health

Depression can take a toll on your physical health. It can have direct effects on your body (such as raising your blood pressure, increasing fat deposits around vital organs, causing digestive problems, straining your heart, etc). It affects your body indirectly because of the unhealthy things you do to de-stress (such as smoking, drinking too much alcohol, comfort eating, etc). While your body can cope with this in the short term, used over long periods to try to cope with depression these will leave you with physical illness as well as worsened depression.

To avoid becoming unwell, it is important for you to address the physical consequences of depression in healthy ways. This means giving up smoking and cutting down on alcohol, caffeine, chocolate and other fatty and sugary foods. It also means adopting healthy approaches to:

- Posture
- Activity
- Sleep
- Diet.

In the longer term, making healthy lifestyle choices in each of these areas will improve your resilience to stress as well as improving your general wellbeing.

Posture

One physical response to stress is for your body to curl in on itself. We evolved to do this in order to coil our muscles (ready to fight or flee) and to protect the vital organs in the chest and abdomen.

While adopting a crouched posture isn't too much of a problem in the short-term, in time it will have a negative impact on your health and wellbeing. You will experience aches and pains in your back, shoulders, neck and head as a result of the tension in the muscles. Your breathing will be impaired by the additional pressure on your lungs and diaphragm. The pressure on your abdomen will also impact on the way your vital organs function.

More subtly, the way you see and interact with the world will change. To appreciate this, try exaggerating the posture by hunching your shoulders and neck forward. Without changing the position, check your field of vision. Now exaggerate an open posture with your back straight, shoulders back and head upright. Check your field of vision again. See the difference?

Taking time regularly to re-adjust your posture and to gently stretch your body can be helpful. If you want to do more, exercise programmes such as Alexander Technique, Pilates and Yoga are particularly helpful for correcting poor posture.

Activity

Depression will leave you feeling exhausted, and often just wanting to lie down or sit in front of the TV. While this is okay in the short-term, it can become a habit. And the less you do, the less you are able to do.

Being physically active is an essential part of healthy living, and has been shown to promote recovery from depression.

Ideally you should try to do something physical to the point that it increases your heart and breathing rate for about 30 minutes a day on most days.

Being physically active need not involve joining a gym or buying expensive sports equipment (although this is fine if you can commit to it). Just taking a half-hour walk at lunch time, doing some work in the garden or tidying around the house counts as physical activity.

If you can engage in activities you enjoy and especially where there is a social element (e.g., going swimming or cycling with a friend) you are much more likely to keep doing them.

Sleep

Poor sleep is both a symptom and a cause of depression. Typically, your sleep will be disrupted in three ways:

- Being unable to get to sleep at night

o Waking and being unable to get back to sleep in the early hours

o Sleeping during the day.

Over time your lack of sleep (and the resulting tiredness) will leave you even more susceptible to depression.

There are many things you can do to improve your sleep and relaxation. As a starting point, you should avoid substances and activities that over-stimulate you (such as coffee, computer games and excess alcohol) in the run up to bedtime. Instead, try to do things that promote sleep and relaxation (such as taking a warm bath, having a milky drink or listening to a relaxation CD). Our *Getting to Sleep* booklet explains this in more detail.

It helps to get into a routine. Try to take 15-20 minutes every day to relax. Find somewhere quiet and comfortable where you won't be disturbed. Try to use the same time and place every day.

Similarly with sleep, try to go to bed at the same time every night. Keep the bedroom free of clutter, and avoid having computers, TVs, phones and (if possible) clocks in the bedroom.

It is important not to try to "catch up" on sleep during the day. This will just leave you unable to sleep at night. Also, try to avoid lying in on the weekend, as this can also disrupt your sleep routine (it has been likened to jet lag).

If sleep and relaxation are particularly difficult for you, you may want to think about trying a complementary therapy like aromatherapy, massage or reflexology. Alternatively, you could join a local tai chi or yoga class.

Diet

There are several ways in which depression affects your diet. Most directly, substances such as alcohol, caffeine, chocolate and sugar contain chemicals that help counteract the effects of stress and anxiety. You may find that you unconsciously reach for food and drink that contain these substances when you are depressed.

Psychologically, you may be inclined to comfort eat as a way of feeling better when you are stressed. You may "treat yourself" to a big bar of chocolate, a pack of cream cakes or a tub of ice cream—this is okay once in a while, but it will affect your weight and your general sense of wellbeing if it becomes a habit.

Depression will deaden your senses of smell and taste. This becomes particularly pronounced for people who develop severe depression. One result of this is that you may begin to choose foods that are heavily flavoured, salty or sweet. In most cases, these foods are unhealthy and will have a negative impact on your wellbeing in the longer-term.

You may also be tempted to opt for foods (simple carbohydrates like sugar and sweets) that give a quick energy burst by increasing your blood sugar levels. However, the energy burst will be short lived, and you will quickly feel tired again. The alternative is to opt for complex carbohydrates (like potatoes, pasta and rice) that increase your energy levels more slowly, but maintain your energy levels for much longer.

There is a range of foods that are thought to improve mood and energy levels (you can find out more in the Life Surfing Booklet *Food & Mood*). However, perhaps more important is learning to eat a balanced diet that is low in fat and high in fibre, with plenty of fruit and vegetables.

Emotional Wellbeing

Depression is not just about external events. It is also to do with the way you respond.

One of the dangers facing you as you become more depressed is that you turn emotions such as guilt, anger, self-blame and hate in upon yourself. This will impact badly on the way you think and act.

Learning to manage and express your feelings in a healthy way will help you to improve your resilience to depression in the longer-term.

The most important thing you can do is talk about your feelings. This doesn't mean opening up to anyone irrespective of whether they want to hear about your feelings. Rather, it means finding a trusted friend or relative who will give you the time and space to express how you are feeling.

In the absence of someone close enough to you for you to feel comfortable about expressing your feelings, there are several alternatives:

Use a helpline such as Community Advice and Listening Line (0800 123 737). If you are in employment, your employer may operate a telephone counselling service. You may also have access to telephone counselling if you have medical insurance.

See if you can access face-to-face counselling. There may be a counsellor based at your local doctors' surgery (although there will most probably be a waiting list). Alternatively, there are many charities that offer counselling in your area. If you have sufficient income, you may want to pay for private counselling—but be aware that the costs can mount up.

Use online social media to interact with people who have similar issues to you.

You might also want to think about engaging in creative activities that may help you express your feelings less directly. Arts, crafts, music and poetry are all ways in which people can express themselves.

Thoughts and Beliefs

The more depressed you become, the more likely you are to develop irrational, unrealistic and often negative thoughts and beliefs. Unfortunately, this is an insidious process that prevents you noticing what is happening.

Unpicking thoughts and beliefs can be difficult to do on your own. This is why it can be helpful to seek counselling or a psychological therapy such as Cognitive Behavioural Therapy (CBT), which can help you develop a more realistic appraisal of your thoughts and beliefs.

You may be able to access psychological therapies through your employer if they have an Employee Assistance Programme (EAP). If you are on benefits but seeking to return to work, you may be able to access CBT via JobCentre Plus.

If you are unable to access face-to-face therapy, there is a computerised programme called *Beating the Blues* that is available through the NHS. There are also several online CBT programmes that can be accessed free of charge.

Core Skills and Abilities

We all have things that we are inherently good at. And the more we engage with the things we are good at, the better our wellbeing. However, our key skills are often dormant or frustrated because of our need to make our way in the world. The need to put food on the table takes precedence over learning and practice for many of us.

This is often compounded by our upbringing, which in turn shapes our self-beliefs. If you come to believe that you will never be an artist or a musician or a writer or a surgeon, etc, then you will never put in the hours of learning and practice needed to turn these latent talents into developed skills.

Some people are fortunate enough to be able to utilise their skills and abilities in their work. However, for many others, this must be done outside work by participating in hobbies or through involvement in community groups.

It can be difficult to identify those of your skills and abilities that are undeveloped or frustrated. However, a starting point is to understand that when someone is fully engaging their skills and abilities, they develop a sense of *flow*—the feeling that everything is happening easily. This is similar to sportspeople who talk about being "in the zone".

Think about times in your life when you have felt like this, and try to remember what you were doing. What were the skills and abilities that you were drawing on? It can help to try to match these to things that you have always wanted to do (including those that you may have told yourself you would never be any good at).

If you can develop and work with your core skills and abilities, you will find that life becomes easier, more enjoyable, and that you are much more resilient in the face of depression.

Lining everything up

The key to long-term wellbeing is to develop healthy approaches to all five of these areas of your being. A person with wellbeing will be socially engaged, physically healthy, aware of her or his emotions, mindful and realistic about his or her thoughts and beliefs, and will be engaging her or his core skills and abilities either through employment, hobbies or through community participation.

In reality, few of us live up to such a high standard. For some, the leap can appear so big that we don't even begin to try.

The important thing is to acknowledge where you are, and work from there. A person who smokes, overeats and drinks too much alcohol is not going to run a marathon any time soon. But they can begin to alter their diet, cut down on the alcohol, and (if they put their mind to it) give up smoking. At the same time, they can go for a walk every evening or do a bit more around the house or in the garden.

Taking things in small, achievable steps is the only way that you can get from where you are to where you want to be. Anything more is just setting yourself up to fail. Try to do too much, and you will just add to the depression that you are trying to manage.

Remember that even a marathon runner doesn't begin by being able to run 26 miles in less than two hours. Like you, they began by taking a single step.

About Life Surfing

Life Surfing is a not-for-profit Community Interest Company that was established to provide a coaching, mentoring and training approach for people experiencing common life problems that can cause stress, anxiety and depression.

Our mission is to help people learn to cope with life without the need to call on over-stretched NHS services that are better deployed to help people with severe mental illness.

Over the years we have found that there is a huge amount that people can do to develop their personal resources and to foster their own wellbeing. In most cases, the real need is for encouragement, support, knowledge and skills.

This is what Life Surfing offers.

We have developed a range of services – one-to-one coaching, training workshops, mentoring groups and a range of publications - to give you the knowledge, skills and motivation needed to address life's issues and overcome stress-related problems in a healthy way, and to promote your long-term personal wellbeing.

For further information, please visit the Life Surfing website:

www.life-surfing.com
info@life-surfing.com

Or you can contact us on: 0300 321 4514 / 07922 537 646

Life Surfing
Box 124, R&R Consulting Centre
41 St. Isan Road
Heath
Cardiff CF14 4LW

Life Surfing is a community interest company limited by guarantee
(07399335) registered in England and Wales